MARY'S
WAY OF THE CROSS

WALKING WITH THE MOTHER OF JESUS

By Irma Pfeifer

Translated and adapted by M. Jean Frisk

Hymn texts by Daniela Raab

Art by Charlie Craig

Pauline
BOOKS & MEDIA
Boston

Library of Congress Cataloging-in-Publication Data

Frisk, M. Jean.
  Mary's Way of the Cross : walking with the mother of Jesus / Irma Pfeifer ;
translated and adapted by M. Jean Frisk ; hymn texts by Daniela Raab.— 1st
English ed.
     p. cm.
  ISBN 0-8198-4838-7 (pbk.)
  1. Stations of the cross—Meditations. 2. Mary, Blessed Virgin, Saint—
Meditations. 3. Motherhood—Religious aspects—Christianity—Meditations. 4.
Devotional literature. I. Pfeifer, Irma. Mit Maria den Kreuzweg gehen. II. Title.
  BX2040.F75 2006
  232.96—dc22

                                                            2005020594

Cover design by Rosana Usselmann

Cover art by Charlie Craig

Originally published on July 12, 1988, in German by the Secretariat of the
Schoenstatt Mothers League, Schönstatt-Verlag, 5414 Vallendar, Germany. Since
then there have been several printings.

Published by Pauline Books & Media, 50 Saint Paul's Avenue, Boston, MA
02130-3491. www.pauline.org.

Printed in the U.S.A.

Pauline Books & Media is the publishing house of the Daughters of St. Paul, an
international congregation of women religious serving the Church with the
communications media.

5 6 7 8 9 10   19 18 17 16 15

FOREWORD

A woman walks with the Mother of Jesus on his way of the cross,
wondering how it was…and is.

*I*n the early 1990s, Irma Pfeifer attended a retreat at
Schoenstatt in Vallendar, overlooking the Rhine River Valley
in Germany. Irma had recently experienced loss and pain in her
personal life. Attending the retreat in this place of natural beau-
ty and peace dedicated to the Blessed Virgin Mary, Irma began
to experience tremendous comfort and strength. Although she
didn't want to share the details of her personal life and family,
during the retreat Irma wrote a series of reflections on the four-
teen Stations of the Cross at the urging of M. Daniela Raab, a
Schoenstatt Sister of Mary responsible for the retreat and for the
Schoenstatt Mothers League at the time.

Irma's Stations are unique in that they converse with
Mary, wondering—mother to mother—what it was like for
Mary to walk with *her* suffering Son. Sister Daniela later com-
plemented the reflections by adding poetic verses inspired by
the familiar Lenten hymn, "At the Cross Her Station Keeping"
(*Stabat Mater Dolorosa*).

By 1991, Irma Pfeifer's work, *Mit Maria den Kreuzweg gehen*
("Walk the Stations of the Cross with Mary"), was well into its
third printing. At the time, nearly 10,000 women belonging to
the Schoenstatt Movement had prayed the Stations and identi-

fied with the questions and the pain experienced by Mary, Mother of Jesus, as she is confronted with the cross.

When I was asked to write a book of reflections on the Way of the Cross with Mary as companion on the journey, as many as forty individuals recommended Pfeifer's work. Finally, by the sheer number of recommendations and several gifts of the booklet itself, I, too, walked these Stations. The result? Amazement! Many of my own thoughts coincided with Irma's—which is perhaps not so amazing at all, since we belong to the same Marian movement within the Church: Schoenstatt.

Founded in 1914, Schoenstatt is a biblically-based spirituality that seeks to walk intimately with Christ as Mary did—in love's covenant communally and individually. For the Mothers League, emphasis is placed on creating a faith-filled, Holy Family atmosphere in life at home and in everyday society.

These Stations, then, are Irma Pfeifer's and M. Daniela Raab's, but they are also mine and yours. They have been translated and adapted for English-speaking pilgrims on Christ's path. In reality, though, they must yet be translated into the life and circumstances of each one who prays them. If the Spirit moves you while praying and reflecting on the words that follow, *do* put down this booklet and write your own Stations. Etch them deeply into your heart.

— M. JEAN FRISK

INTRODUCTION

Walking the Way of the Cross with Mary

With *Mary*—what does that mean? Do we put Mary in Christ's place, or by speaking to Mary, do we detract from Christ's redemptive suffering? He alone is our Savior!

Those who ponder these texts will find the answer. Mary doesn't take Christ's place—she takes *our* place. She embodies to the fullest the vocation that Jesus Christ entrusted to each one of us: "He called the crowd with his disciples, and said to them, 'If any want to become my followers, let them deny themselves and take up their cross and follow me'" (Mk 8:34).

A hard saying! Anyone who has suffered destiny's blows knows that to love the cross for its own sake is impossible. It would break us.

Mary walks another way. She loves Christ passionately and totally. Her love made her ready for anything and everything, as long as she could be more profoundly one with him and could serve his work. Her love urged her to suffer the way of the cross with her Son. This is how she fully matured.

Now she helps us to master the anxieties and limitations we encounter on our life's way of the cross, and through them to grow in love. Those who walk the Stations of the Cross with Mary will experience them as a path of blessings, as a liberating journey on the way to God.

Suggestions for Use

The following meditations can be used for personal reflection as well as for communal prayer. For groups, it may be helpful to plan a brief period of silent reflection after the text is read aloud. If the meditations take place in a church, soft background organ variations, such as "At the Cross Her Station Keeping," could be a helpful bridge between stations. The devotion can be shortened where necessary and appropriate by selecting just one or several individual stations.

PRAYER TO BEGIN
THE STATIONS

*M*ary, Mother of our Redeemer and our Mother! You were the first to be with him on this earth. From the moment of his indwelling in you, to his birth when you took him into your arms, to his first journey to his Father's house, throughout his hidden and public life, you were his companion—with him, loving him, centered on him.

At the ultimate point of redemption, his suffering and death, you were there. Now, too, you are called to stand at his side, for his redemptive work continues in every age. We would like to walk with you for a while on your journey through the ages. Don't allow us to remain standing on the sidelines like uninvolved spectators. Point out the way, each step and implication, as you did so long ago.

Teach us to be peaceful, to remember that Easter is at the end. Free us of useless thoughts. For just these few minutes, help us to forget the many things we have to do. Open the eyes of our hearts so that love alone is what we see behind all of this. Yes, Mary, help us to see everything with our hearts and, like you, to ponder with our hearts what we don't understand.

You who once by God were chosen
bore the Lord for our redemption;
you may stand now at his side.
You could walk with him each station,
then and now, each generation,
close to Jesus to the last.

UNJUSTLY CONDEMNED

𝒱. We adore you, O Christ, and we bless you.

ℛ. Because by your holy cross
you have redeemed the world.

Your Son stands before the court. He is not guilty, but he is condemned to death—he who did only good, who healed the sick and awakened the dead to life, who wanted only to love! You are his Mother. You know him and you cannot comprehend what has happened here. Can't they see?

You experience how Jesus is taunted, insulted, betrayed. You search the crowd for his friends. There is no one. Have they all abandoned him? They were there when he was chained, then they ran. Sadly you note that no one defends him now. And he is silent. Yet in spite of chains, he is free.

You can do nothing for him, not even to go to him. But at this moment you are closer to him than ever before. Mary, you are his Mother, our Mother, my Mother. You know how afraid I am of others' opinions. You know how quickly I tend to judge others without knowing all the facts. I too look on when injustice takes place. I stand on the sidelines where it doesn't touch me. I wait, detached, as if I were watching just another film. I hope that someone else will take the initiative. Mary, what would you do in my place if you had the chance? Can you help me to think before I accuse? To remember Jesus at that moment and not to expose and condemn my neighbors by uncontrolled and unnecessary talk? Help me to discover God in others. Like you, help me to deeply, personally encounter behind all happenings—even this—the God of life, love, and justice.

You must watch him stand condemned.
Pain and terror—you alone seem to care.
Not one friend defends your good Son.
Help my words be ever truthful,
never testifying falsely,
even if I stand alone.

YOUR SON
TAKES THE CROSS

V. We adore you, O Christ, and we bless you.

R. Because by your holy cross
you have redeemed the world.

*H*e drags his cross for love of us. You are his Mother, but you cannot change a thing. You can only accompany him, be close to him even if only from a distance, and show that like him you are ready to fulfill the Father's will. Were you there when he told the strangers that his hour had come to be glorified? "Very truly, I tell you, unless a grain of wheat falls into the earth and dies, it remains just a single grain; but if it dies, it bears much fruit" (Jn 12:24). Did you hear when he told them, "Now my soul is troubled. And what should I say?—'Father, save me from this hour'? No, it is for this reason that I have come to this hour. Father, glorify your name" (Jn 12:27).

Mary, somehow he understood, he knew the Father's love like no other before him. But did you grasp it at this moment? After Jesus, you carry the heaviest cross ever placed on human shoulders, for you knew like no other that he, your child, came from God and was the Father's Son. Your love for him makes you able to bear this incredible pain in your own utter help-lessness.

How often I try to make things easier for myself! Mary, won't you teach me to bear my cross with the inner joy that committed love brings? My cross is meant for me and for no one else. It is so hard to stick it out and endure the long haul. Walking here with you who are Mother and sister to me, the journey begins to make sense. Your quiet love, joined to my longing, helps me see his suffering face in my cross. It's almost as if you carry my cross for me. I trust that you will teach me to discover God's love directing my life in every situation, just as you found it so in yours. You expect from me only my readiness to continue the journey. Daily, hourly.

Even when the others turn from you,
nothing tears you from the Savior,
your own beloved Son.
You will walk each station, no matter
where it leads.
Help me walk this path, each twisting
and turning,
grateful for the love you're sharing.
Help me to bear my cross with love.

YOU SEE HIM FALL

𝒱. We adore you, O Christ, and we bless you.

ℛ. Because by your holy cross
you have redeemed the world.

*T*he hours in the garden, the betrayal, the hearing, the scourging—it is all too much for your Son. He walks slower. His hands fail to serve him. It is beyond his strength, and you sense what is about to happen. He falls to the ground.

Mary, you have never experienced him like this: your strong, young Son trained in the carpenter's trade, trained to carry heavy beams that his hands would fashion with sure grip. *Will he make it now?* you ask yourself. You know that he has taken more upon himself than just this wooden beam. It is his merciful love for us that gives him the strength to stand again, to take firmer hold of his cross, and to carry it further. He will walk this path to the end—for us.

You know only too well how often I fail each day. How I dread and detest my cross! I often think I won't have the strength to bear it another minute longer, let alone a lifetime. Again and again I stumble and fall under the burden of my own shortcomings. Help me to consider how to take my cross up again and to see it differently. Teach me to have patience with myself and with anyone who stumbles, who makes mistakes, who falls.

To lift up the weak,
to give them his strength,
your Son chose lowliness.
When suffering presses me to the earth,
stand by my side as you stood by his.

Let his redeeming grace flow through your heart
  to warm me,
so that I, too, may bear witness to the fruitfulness
  of his grace
and share his love with others.

YOU MEET HIM
FACE TO FACE

𝒱. We adore you, O Christ, and we bless you.

ℛ. Because by your holy cross
you have redeemed the world.

You know this moment means farewell—perhaps for a long time. What might have taken place in your heart during these minutes? You long to hold him, to comfort him—like you did the times he skinned his knees at play. This is surely the hardest day of your life. You let him go—for us, for this world so in need of mercy. Aching, brokenhearted love urges you to endure this appalling suffering with him. When I see your steadfast love, I know that all those who have to suffer similar things can find consolation and strength in you.

Jesus returns your gaze. Does he see a *why* in your eyes? Couldn't he work a miracle now? He worked so many for others. He worked the Cana miracle for you. He raised the widow's dead son for her. Couldn't he change things now so you could go home together and live a simple, good life?

Like him, you don't want anything to hinder the Father's plan of redemption. To endure it and triumph, Jesus must take onto himself unimaginable human suffering. I know you wanted to be his servant forever, but, Mary, did you realize that the Son you bore would rise again? So did you wait to see what God still planned to do?

Did your silent, compassionate love give him strength to go on? You gaze at one another. These seconds speak more than many words. This is how it ought to be for us. Every day there are such encounters. With your divine Son will you, too, walk beside me, look at me deep down, return my *why* with your gentle presence? When we look at one another, let it be as valuable as a long conversation. When others look at me and I at them, how beautiful it would be if we saw the face of Christ reflected there, just as you reflected it!

Your eyes communicate to your Son
that with him you will do what the Father asks —
till life is totally given for the friend.
I would like to join with him,
one with you to find the Father and the infinite
    mystery of his love,
one with you to hold lovingly still without
    question.

SIMON HELPS JESUS

℣. We adore you, O Christ, and we bless you.

℟. Because by your holy cross
you have redeemed the world.

*S*imon is forced to help your Son carry his burden. How gladly you, his Mother, would have liked to take Simon's place. A stranger shoulders the precious burden. Your help is not required. Yet love is inventive. You discover another way to help. Unnoticed and quiet—the inconspicuous pattern of your love —is also your way to suffer.

Mother, show me where I can help, where I am needed— not being insistent or pushy, obtrusive or noisy, but being quietly understanding and compassionate, even if it means I can only share by bringing others' needs to God in prayer. Let me be a welcoming, receiving "space" where others can confidently place their worries and concerns without my own needs filling up all the room; a Simon who helps others to bear their cross.

If you cannot turn the destiny of your Son with
     your own hands,
you nevertheless ease his burden by your quiet
     presence.
Make me free of timid hesitation,
free to see and serve where it is best to do so,
that my heart, carried by love,
may embrace his cross.

VERONICA

𝒱. We adore you, O Christ, and we bless you.

ℛ. Because by your holy cross
you have redeemed the world.

*T*he woman holding the cloth doesn't bother about the crowd. She breaks through the wall of insensitivity and mediocrity that surrounds her. Her courage is amazing. Mary, even in your anguish did your heart experience a wave of joy at seeing this loving gesture? Was it as if you personally had been helped? Here was someone who endangered her own life to help your Son. From a distance you look on. You see that there are still some who will stand by Jesus. And this consoles you in your profound sorrow. Veronica cannot free Jesus from his cross, but she doesn't stop there. She still shows she cares. She does what is possible for her to do. Jesus looks at her and lets her know how precious even a seemingly insignificant service can be.

Mother, give me courage, too, to help with the means at my disposal—be they ever so trivial in the eyes of others. Greatness shows itself in little things. Small services can be a sign of genuine love. A kind word, a friendly look, a gesture—these are the little things that can transform hearts, heal rifts, fight depression, change selfishness into a love that recognizes the need of the neighbor. How I long to be like Veronica and have his face etched in my memory forever!

Genuine, courageous strength,
confidently, gently challenging,
finds ways to show faithfulness
to Jesus' word and way.
Teach me in faithful love to stand by him,
the only measure: love.

GOD PRESSED
TO THE EARTH

℣. We adore you, O Christ, and we bless you.

℟. Because by your holy cross
you have redeemed the world.

Your Son falls to the ground again, experiencing the limits of his strength. In reparation for human pride, he allows his human nature to suffer more deeply than any other person. He places the highest demands on himself—does not give up, but lifts himself up and goes on. Love urges him to drink the chalice to the full. He wants to do more than *this and no more,* for his love never says, *I've had enough.*

I am blocked by the fear of falling, the fear that I won't make it, that things won't turn out as I hoped. True, I want to carry my cross, but I want to determine its weight myself so that I won't fall and look bad before others. And when I fall, as we all must, I have so many excuses ready for why I've fallen.

Mother, teach me to comprehend that my suffering, my falling and rising, can become a blessing for others—if I remain simple, humble, honest; if I *own* my humanness truthfully. Stop me when I am tempted to turn away from his torn face and say, *I've had enough.*

His strength has left him again.
Still he wants to dare the ultimate.
He never says, "I've had enough!"
You see him with his face crushed to the dust;
want to give him everything,
want to cover his bleeding with love.
If only I could be you—another Mary—
living only for him to my last breath.

THE WEEPING WOMEN

V. We adore you, O Christ, and we bless you.

R. Because by your holy cross
you have redeemed the world.

*I*n his own unspeakable agony, Jesus hears the complaints and wailing of the women who follow him. They experience painfully, deeply, the suffering of your Son, but they cannot grasp it or see through it.

You know the compassionate heart of your Son. Do you sense that he will stop to console these women? That is his way. He consoles others and doesn't think of himself, but he also makes them aware that the real reason for sorrow is sin—theirs, mine, sins of the children's children.

Your beloved Son became your example in all things. You, too, console the afflicted. You, too, bring light to those who live in error. Many persons down through the ages have asked you to teach them how to love him as you did. Teach me, too.

Mother, so often I walk by and just don't see! Help me to never intentionally pass by the suffering of others, but I also don't want to intrude where silence is the better gift. Teach me to distinguish what form my compassion is to take, to console others even on my own down days. Pity is appalling. Empathy alone is not enough. And no one is served when we accuse a third party or place the blame on others. *We* have to change. Each one. Here and now. Let me learn from you what true consolation is. It is more than clichéd expressions of sympathy—the usual things we say when we are uncomfortable in the face of another's loss and pain. Mary, show me how you do it; how I, too, can help others experience your Son's merciful love.

Your Jesus turns toward the women.
He speaks kindly, clearly.
Do not cry for me, he says, but for yourselves and
    your children.
The genuine reason to cry lies in our sins.
Mother, help me to look deeper,
not to gullibly trust in appearances,
but to consider the consequences of these actions.
Let goodness and kindness be victorious in me.

THIRD FALL

𝒱. We adore you, O Christ, and we bless you.

𝓡. Because by your holy cross
you have redeemed the world.

You watch your beloved child grow weaker with every step. You see how he falls, exhausted—at the limits of his physical strength. How excruciating for him! How agonizing for you as his Mother to have to see this without being able to intervene! Powerlessness! This is what it means! Ancient legends tell us you fainted here—that you felt his weakness in your own limbs and stumbled to the ground. I wonder, did anyone help you as you longed to help him?

How shall this go on? Yet you continue to believe. Far away, in a time long past, you heard the words, "For nothing will be impossible with God" (Lk 1:37). He gets up again. He knows what is still possible when it all seems unthinkable to the rest of us.

I fall so often each and every day, cannot manage much in life, and often imagine that my cross is harder to bear than my neighbor's. The cross of personal weakness and guilt presses me down. Mother, you went through this with his wounds etched in your heart. Walk beside me! Help me find shelter and mercy, so that I will draw strength to stand up again and follow him, no matter where it takes me. Teach me in turn how to be close to those who have fallen next to me. Teach me to understand that I don't have to do everything myself. Ultimately, all of us on the journey together may place our full trust in him who embraces us with his compassionate love.

God's power will win in the end.
You trust in his omnipotence,
even now when he lies helpless on the ground
before us.
When my strength dwindles,
my only hope is to be wrapped in his strength
and warmed by the presence you share,
so that Eternal Love's power may be victorious
in me.

STRIPPED

$V\!.$ We adore you, O Christ, and we bless you.

$R\!.$ Because by your holy cross
you have redeemed the world.

*D*id you weave the garment they tore from his lashed and bleeding body? Did you recall how he liked his privacy—so pure, so strong? True, he never lived in luxury and comfort, but here they took the last thing he had on earth, his clothing. The executioners take no note of their victim's honor, nor of that fine feeling of human privacy. Nothing may belong to him anymore—not exteriorly, not interiorly. He allows himself to be made poor that we may become rich. One could hardly be more lowly or poor. Surrounded by gawking crowds, he feels this humiliation burning worse than all his wounds. It is true that they—and we—make sport of Jesus, but no one can injure his greatness. No one can rob him of his godly dignity.

Mary, you know how frequently human dignity is under-valued, neglected, even despised in our time—the dignity of women, the dignity of unborn children, the dignity of prison-ers and the elderly. Help me to protect them whenever I have the opportunity. Teach me how to stand up for the honor of others, but remain calm myself if someone deprives me of the respect and recognition I think are rightly mine.

Whatever people permit themselves to do
cannot rob him of his honor.
He remains King—then and now.
You seek to increase his honor.
This is why you continue to come among us—

a tradition you carry on through the ages.
Let me walk with you, Mary!
Teach me to pray as he taught us,
"Father, all glory be yours" (cf. Jn 12:28; 17:1, 4).

THEY NAIL HIM TO THE CROSS

℣. We adore you, O Christ, and we bless you.

℟. Because by your holy cross
you have redeemed the world.

*A*s Mother, can you look at this scene without breaking down? I hear the ringing blows and cringe. I stop my ears and look away. Was it that way for you?

You miss no blow of the hammer, no taunting mockery. You know the inner anguish of your Son, the isolation and loneliness he must endure in the midst of this raucous cruelty. There is no going back. He is fastened to the cross, and again you are overwhelmed in the realization that you can do nothing for him except be with him until this terrible thing is over.

My inability to love, drowned in selfishness and self-pity, nails your Son to the cross day after day. When I insist on doing things my way and only my way, I drill the nails deeper into his wounds. I know it—I am forever *reacting,* following the impulses of my first reaction, not pausing, pondering, praying to know God's will and plan through this event or that person. Forgive me! Give me the strength to bear the "nails" in my life as atonement for the nails he bore.

Even though your soul quakes,
you want to share everything with him,
be with him during his passion and death,
be with him at the hour of our redemption.
Mary, help me to see the whole picture,
to find the horizon beyond myself,
to stand by him as you did,
to live the way you lived.

HE DIES FOR US

𝒱. We adore you, O Christ, and we bless you.

ℛ. Because by your holy cross
you have redeemed the world.

*H*e speaks still. Word after word is pressed into your motherly heart. Somehow you sense that the yes you said long ago wasn't said in vain. From the cross he gives you to us as Mother.

Your motherly love, motherly care, is to extend to us. This is your Son's final mandate, his farewell greeting. Yes, this is his final gift before he completes the redemptive death for us. With him, you give yourself to the Father as he surrenders his life, "Father, into your hands..." (Lk 23:46).

Mary, could you fathom the whole *why* of his death any more than I can? Could you *really* give your yes as fully as he gave his? The ancients tell us that you longed for this redemptive hour in the fullness of your own love. And it is true that you stood at his side to the bitter end.

Mary! You, living gift of our Lord and Savior! Make me ready—like you—to sacrifice what I love most, if the Father wills it, if it may become one small share in bringing faith, hope, and healing love to those around me. Help me to pray courageously, "Take from me my very self if it disturbs this love."

He whom you once gave human life
wants to give you to us as Mother
—his testament of love—
that our doxology will never end:

Glory be joyfully given to the Father
through Christ with Mary, highly praised,
in the Holy Spirit full of splendor
from the universe now and for all eternity.

HE IS LAID
IN YOUR ARMS

℣. We adore you, O Christ, and we bless you.

℟. Because by your holy cross
you have redeemed the world.

Now for the last time you hold him in your arms. You are alone with him and with the Father. Your thoughts wander back thirty years. His death—like his birth—takes place in conditions of extreme need and contempt. He whom you carried in your arms as a child now lies before you gruesomely executed. You meditate on his wounds, trace your finger over the places where the thorns penetrated. I, too, share guilt for this. Have you forgiven us who mistreated him this way? Your kind, quiet gentleness speaks acceptance and forgiveness. Pray for us! Pray for me!

Tell me, Mother, what I can do in response to his love, your love. Show me what sacrifice he expects of me. Help me to bear my present pain in atonement for my sins and the sins of others.

Silently surrendered to the Father,
you sacrifice the life of your Son
in heroic renunciation and acceptance.
Your faith finds a glimmer of light in
*   the darkness,*
and allows you to see him who shatters
*   the darkness*
of death and night and horror.

HE IS LAID
IN A GRAVE

℣. We adore you, O Christ, and we bless you.

℟. Because by your holy cross
you have redeemed the world.

*I*nscrutable moment! Strong, serving hands take his body from you. Now the external separation cannot be avoided. His presence gone, loneliness and abandonment must have filled your heart. Do the others standing by you, his friends, now think that everything is over, senseless, for nothing? Not you! You believe in God's mercy; you sang of his mercy and continue to sing it from generation to generation. Your heart again finds peace, for his mercy will somehow show itself from age to age. Even now! God makes no mistakes. You trust this, your yes remains, you are totally given to the Father.

Blessed Mother, Christ-bearer, I admire your strength and ask you to intercede and obtain this kind of faithful strength for me. How often I pray so routinely, *Your will be done....* But do I really mean it? How hard it is for me to grasp the Father's will! He awaits my yes, no matter what happens to me.

How often we bury human hope! We can't seem to recognize God's wise guidance. Mary, teach us to trust that God makes no mistakes.

All your loving, wishing, thinking,
melts down, merges—one with the Father's
    plan of love.
Help me to quiet all my longing,
that the Father's loving will
may be fulfilled in me
and in those I love.

CONCLUDING PRAYER

*M*ary, Mother of God and my own Blessed Mother, it is hard to comprehend, but how you must have pleased the Father in this hour of suffering! He expected much of you. Indeed, you did justice to his demands. You stuck it out. You stayed close to your Son, in spite of physical distance and helplessness. You were united with him in the midst of your own inner agony.

In God there is no separation. No one may divide this Son and this Mother! This is the plan. The suffering of your Son and how you accompanied him is always an example, a source of strength and consolation for me. You want to be close to me when the Father places great demands on me, too. Walking with you, I learn how to see and do things his way.

Take me along every day on your path at the side of your Son. Take me along to the real and most beautiful goal of our lives. With Jesus, the Christ, take us to the Father, for according to the Savior's word this is each one's destiny.

Mother, what you bore
urges me to say a loving thank you.
You endured suffering not for him alone—

yes, for him in the first place—
but also for me.
If only I could walk like you through life,
a thanksgiving gift in return.

My path leads homeward to the Father
where you are at home,
where your divine Son reigns in glory,
where the Holy Spirit fills every vast void,
including empty human hearts,
where love and joy have no end.
Let each step lead me there.

BOOKS & MEDIA

The Daughters of St. Paul operate book and media centers at the following addresses. Visit, call, or write the one nearest you today, or find us at www.pauline.org.

CALIFORNIA

3908 Sepulveda Blvd, Culver City, CA 90230	310-397-8676
935 Brewster Avenue, Redwood City, CA 94063	650-369-4230
5945 Balboa Avenue, San Diego, CA 92111	858-565-9181

FLORIDA

145 S.W. 107th Avenue, Miami, FL 33174	305-559-6715

HAWAII

1143 Bishop Street, Honolulu, HI 96813	808-521-2731

ILLINOIS

172 North Michigan Avenue, Chicago, IL 60601	312-346-4228

LOUISIANA

4403 Veterans Memorial Blvd, Metairie, LA 70006	504-887-7631

MASSACHUSETTS

885 Providence Hwy, Dedham, MA 02026	781-326-5385

MISSOURI

9804 Watson Road, St. Louis, MO 63126	314-965-3512

NEW YORK

64 W. 38th Street, New York, NY 10018	212-754-1110

SOUTH CAROLINA

243 King Street, Charleston, SC 29401	843-577-0175

TEXAS

Currently no book center; for parish exhibits or outreach evangelization, contact: 210-569-0500, or SanAntonio@paulinemedia.com, or P.O. Box 761416, San Antonio, TX 78245

VIRGINIA

1025 King Street, Alexandria, VA 22314	703-549-3806

CANADA

3022 Dufferin Street, Toronto, ON M6B 3T5	416-781-9131